7 Steps for

Minimalism

Declutter:

How To Create A

Remarkable Home And Kiss

Your Trash Goodbye

Renae K. Elsworth

Table of Contents

Description

If you are tired of the clutter in your home, the stress it causes you, and the way it projects your image to the world, then *7 Steps for Minimalism Declutter: How to Create a Remarkable Home and Kiss Your Trash Goodbye* is the book that you have been waiting for.

Sometimes we find the process of decluttering to be difficult because we hold mysterious attachments to items that we do not really need, and in some cases, do not even want to keep. Learn the reasons behind these attachments, and how to detach yourself from things. You will find that with fewer items in your home, the special things really shine, and you will have the opportunity to truly cherish what is important to you.

You will be able to get started on your journey to declutter and create the home you have always envisioned. You will be able to get tips to declutter and strategies for organizing to put you on the right track toward achieving your vision of your home at its best. Discover new uses for digital photos, and try out tips for organization stations and aesthetically pleasing decor arrangements to see what works best for you in your home.

Once you declutter, organize, and create your way to a happier, more remarkable home, you will want to maintain your new mindset and keep the old habits away. Take some helpful hints at the ways to form new habits. Make donating unneeded possessions fun! Learn the questions you need to ask yourself before making new purchases. Never allow the clutter to overtake your home and your serenity ever again.

The new, calmer, happier, and less stressed version of yourself will be projected to others around you through your clearer mind and your remarkable home. Can't wait to begin your new phase in life?

In this book, you will find:

- The secret of why you feel emotional attachments to physical possessions.
- Ways to detach emotionally from the clutter, based on why you have kept it.
- Getting started with ridding your home of garbage and unnecessary clutter.
- The reason why you are able to truly cherish your possessions when you have less.
- How to rejuvenate your mind when you are at home in order to present the best version of yourself to the world?
- The best way to determine which items you truly cherish and which ones are wreaking havoc on your home environment.
- The best ways to maintain the correct mindset to keep a clean and relaxing home.
- Tips on organizing your possessions.
- Ways to reclaim time and space in your home.

- Tips to develop the home environment you want.

- How can you break the clutter habit once and for all?

- Tips on retraining your mind to maintain a clutter-free home.

- Ways to incorporate responsibility in the whole family.

- New uses for digital photos.

- Ideas to display knick-knacks and mementos for a truly remarkable home.

- Strategies to keep the clutter at bay.

- *And more…*

Introduction

Congratulations on downloading *7 **Steps for Minimalism Declutter: How to Create a Remarkable Home and Kiss Your Trash Goodbye*** and thank you for doing so. Many people all over the world are finding it empowering and life-changing to declutter their homes. They learn along the way that the clutter and useless items in their homes negatively impact their minds, and therefore, their lives. While changing your mindset and decluttering your home, you too can find the magic in having the home of your dreams and see the effect of a tidy and clutter-free home on all aspects of your life.

The following chapters will help to explain why attachment to physical items can really do more harm than good. You will learn strategies that will help you detach yourself from unnecessary things while developing deeper connections to those things that really do matter in your life. You will be able to discover which items truly hold special meaning, how to separate those from the rest and kiss the trash goodbye.

You will learn tips for getting the home and life you want and deserve. Once you are on your way to happiness with less clutter around to cloud your way, you will learn how to keep yourself on the right track. Strategies and mantras can help you to continue on your new path to a clutter-free life and keep you from slipping back into old habits.

There are plenty of books on this subject on the market, so thanks again for choosing this one! Every effort was made to ensure it is full of as much useful information as possible. Please enjoy!

Chapter 1: Detachment and Attachment of Things

One of the biggest sources of continued stress in life, and one that may seem insurmountable, often presents itself in the form of a disorganized and messy home. It can be so frustrating to put in the utmost effort but never get anywhere close to the calming home you desire. Your home should be a welcoming oasis of calm that you can enter at the end of each long and arduous day to fully relax and unwind. Yet, if you find messes, chaos, and disorganization in your home, the opposite will occur. When there is no welcoming spot, there will be no time to unravel at the end of a long day and just be. You will not have the chance to rest and relax. There will be no time to de-stress and prepare yourself for your next busy day. This is not good for you mentally, emotionally, or physically. One of the simplest ways to make a dramatic change is to start with some simple decluttering of items that are not needed. Understandably, this can be quite difficult to do when there is an attachment to the physical items you possess.

Attachment of Things

It is a part of human nature to want to hold onto the things you have spent your life gathering. This is why so many people have collections. To be able to declutter, you must first learn why you have an attachment to so many physical items. As long as you feel this emotional attachment, it can be very difficult, painful, and even impossible to let go of some of the things that are causing you the very sense of chaos in your life that you want to avoid. You can get in our own way of trying to create a remarkable and calming environment in your home. You must learn to detach from physical things, and in doing so, you need to learn the reasons behind your attachments in the first place.

You may have a particular item that sparks a special memory. When you see that item, it may trigger the memory and cause you happiness. It is not a bad thing to keep some of these items, but you must remember that you will have the memory regardless of the physical possession of such items. You do not necessarily need to keep the physical item as a reminder. Sometimes, there is a whole group of items that relate to one memory. In this case, it is not necessary to physically hold onto all of these things in order to have a nice memory. You must learn to choose items that are most important to you.

You may feel that you worked hard to purchase or own a particular item. These things can be difficult to eliminate from our homes because they cost us something, be it in the form of money, time, or energy. If hard work was put in, an item will hold that hard work as part of its meaning, and an attachment is formed in that way. You must be able to separate the effort from the item, and only keep what truly has a use for you in the present.

Some things come into our homes in the form of gifts. Attachments are often formed to these items because we connect the item with the person who gave us the gift. You may even feel as if you are betraying the person who gave it to you if you do not keep it. These items may also hold a memory. It can be very difficult to let go of things that were given to us by someone we hold dear, especially if it was given in commemoration of a special day or event in our lives. Gifts, cards, mementos, and even hand-me-downs can fall into this category of attachment.

The last category of attachment contains two types of items. The first is the type of items that you have had for a long time. Sometimes it can be really hard to let go of things, not because they have any particular value to you, but because you have had them for a long time. The second type often goes hand in hand with the first. These are the objects that you may tend to personify. Many times, if you have had an item for a long time, you may tend to lend it human characteristics. You may feel bad about letting something go because you imagine it will have hurt feelings. You may feel that you were well served by a particular item and that you will betray it by removing it from your life.

Detachment

Now that you have learned a little bit about some of the ways that you can hold an emotional attachment to physical items, let's discuss how you can learn detachment. In learning to detach yourself from things, you are not becoming a cold or ungrateful person. You are actually becoming a better person who does not need things. You will instead shift your focus from things to people, memories, and other sources of joy in your life. You will feel a lightness both in your home and in yourself when you are able to practice detachment from things.

The first step in detachment is realizing that you cannot let your life be controlled by things. You have to look deep within yourself and really think. Do you want all of these things that you have? Do you want to continue to deal with the chaos and disorganization you find yourself in? Or do you want a calm and peaceful home that you dream of? The things that you possess do not make you who you are as a person. You are not the sum of your possessions. You have your own value as a person.

Next, realize that everything you own must have value in your life. Value can be found in many ways. You may wish to keep things that are useful to you, things that hold a very special memory, or even because they are just pretty. For whatever reason something is important to you, make sure that there is value in that item and not just attachment.

If something that you currently own has no value to you, you do not need it. It is currently standing in the way of your goals and adding to your chaos, your stress, and your inability to have the remarkable home you crave. These are the things that bring you down. You must make the conscious choice to detach from these things.

Think about the items in your life. You can probably make a quick mental list of five things that you hold dear and know the reasons why you would keep them. If you take a quick walk through your home, you will probably also be able to quickly gather five items that have no meaning for you. They are just there, in your home, sucking up space and happiness. These are the types of items from which you can detach. These will be the first type of items you will start to let go of as you learn some tips for decluttering your space.

Your mantra from this chapter is, "I am more than my possessions. My things do not make me who I am as a person."

Chapter 2: Keeping Things Does Not Mean Cherishing Them

Now that you have learned about all of the various ways in which you can hold emotional attachments to the items found in your home, as well as how to allow yourself to detach from these items, it is important to take this sentiment just a step further. You should now have a better understanding of why you have a hard time letting things go. It is time to think about all of the things that you currently own and give deep thought to whether they truly add value to your life. You will learn the truth about possessing items versus cherishing them.

When you own many things, the items that are truly special to you may be brushed aside, or even lost in the clutter. The special things do not have a chance to shine. Just because you keep things, does not mean that you are cherishing them. You may feel that by keeping gifts and hand me down items, you are proving how much you cherish the person from whom they came. You can cherish the person without keeping the items. Keeping them does not equate cherishing them. The same is true of things that you hold onto just because you have had them for a long time or because they saw you through difficult circumstances. Holding on to things for any of these reasons is more likely to burden you than to allow you to cherish your possessions.

It is easier to appreciate items when you have less of them. When you own less, the things that you do possess will be more cherished and can be treated as the important items that they are. As an example, think of the sand at a beach. Picture all of the things that you own as tiny grains of sand on that stretch of beach. With so many unnecessary items, you will never be able to locate one item that is special. You will probably not even know where to look. It would be completely overwhelming. You would have a lot of possessions to be able to fill the space, but they would not be special. You would not be able to cherish the items that were special. You would be better off in having fewer items that truly hold a special meaning than to own a lot that really are not unique or special to you. Instead of having an entire beach full of grains of sand, you could keep just the best and most important things. Think of these items as the seashells. You must be able to sift through all of the sand to be able to locate the seashells that add value and importance to your life.

To start sorting through all the extra sand, a key idea is that if something causes you to feel happy, it is worthy of a place in your life and in your home. If it causes you to feel burdened to have it in your possession, it is not worthy of a place in your life and home. One of the real issues with owning too much is that your possessions begin to take over your life. They take over the physical space in your home. They take over your mental and emotional stability. They begin to own you, instead of you owning them, and this definitely does not lead to cherishing the things that are in your life. Instead, you feel overwhelmed and stressed.

If you have boxes of old mementos or junk stored away in your attic or basement, they are not serving any real purpose. They are only taking up space. They are only causing you stress and anxiety. They are not things that you truly admire, or they would not be stored away. If something no longer has value, it is not worthy of your time or your space. You can keep the memories while getting rid of the physical clutter. The things that make the cut and stay in your life will be much more meaningful. All of your possessions will be useful and cherished. They will all have their own place, and the clutter will decrease. You will be less stressed. You will be able to cherish and display the things you truly love. You will have more joy in your life and feel more contentment within your home. You will be well on your way to having the remarkable, simple, aesthetically pleasing and relaxing home that you desire.

By sorting through your possessions and differentiating between trash and treasure, you are taking back control of your home and your life. You are basically communicating to yourself and to others in the world what is important to you. On top of this, you will have the benefit of a home with a pleasant appearance. Your time spent on cleaning and tidying will decrease. Never again will you have to rush about, stowing things in closets and cupboards because you are expecting visitors. All of this stems from having less and being able to cherish the items that you do possess. You

16

can show the world—or at least all the visitors to your home—exactly what is important to you and also present the best version of yourself through the clean, pleasant, and remarkable environment in which you live.

Let's take a look at what it may mean for you to sort out the items that you cherish and kiss the rest goodbye. You will have more space. All the things that you discover you can happily part with, will no longer be taking up coveted space in your home. You may find yourself with more time on your hands. You might be spending less time tidying things up. You may be spending less time searching for items in the clutter that you used to have. You will have better mental focus and carry less stress. Living without disarray and clutter can completely change your life. Having less means that there is less to keep track of, less to care for, and less to clean. You will be surprised at how much better you will feel when things are decluttered and better organized. Finally, you may find that you are more flexible than you realize. You may discover that you do not actually mind having people over at your home. You might even be up for guests to drop by without a lot of notice. This will be because you do not have to worry about the mess. You can be confident that your remarkable home is projecting an image to the guests of your true self. You will be confident that the things you cherish will do the talking for you in explaining who you are and what is important to you.

Your mantra from this chapter is, "I will take control of my home and my possessions. Keeping things does not mean that I am cherishing them. I will keep only the things I truly admire. The rest no longer has power over me."

Chapter 3: What Is in Your Mind Reflects into the Outer World

You project to the world an image of yourself. This image is a result of what is going on in your mind and in your life. Everyone wants to be seen as the best possible version of themselves. The issue here is that if you are living your life in chaos and discontent due to having too many things, this chaos, disorganization, and discontent are what you will project to others. However, this does not have to be the case. You can make a change.

Psychologists have performed multiple studies and have found that disorganization can lead to anxiety. The reasons behind this are actually fairly simple. It is well explained with the use of a simple exercise.

Think of a typical morning in your life as you wake up and get ready for the day. Reflect on the first things that you see as you open your eyes. Do they give you an impression of calmness or stress? When you move to the bathroom to start your day, is everything exactly where you anticipate it to be? Or do you have to search for your facial cleanser or your comb? When you move to your closet, is everything easily accessible or do you now need to hunt for matching socks? When moving on to the kitchen, can you immediately make your breakfast or your coffee? Or are you greeted by the chaos of unopened mail, loads of jars, or a missing mug? Are you able to quickly gather your keys, wallet, and cell phone? Do you have to search for the things you need to leave your home? At the end of this exercise, do you feel anxious or serene? If you feel anxious, just remember this was just a simulation of the first hour or so of your day. You still have to arrive at work, complete all of your necessary tasks, and then go back home to go through your evening routine. Reflect on how this first hour of your morning will have an effect on the rest of your day. It could be calm and serene, or it could be stressful and harried. It is quite easy to understand how disorganization can lead to anxiety.

When you are not content, you are not able to project calmness, serenity, contentedness, or happiness. Instead, you will project stress, vulnerability, sadness, or irritability. You will project chaos and distractedness. When your home environment causes you to feel stressed and unable to relax, this carries over into your mind. You feel disorganized with your home and possessions, and so your thoughts and actions are disorganized. When trying to project the best image of yourself to others, this is most likely not what you have in mind. Imagine how much more orderly and peaceful your life could be if you have fewer things. You will see only the things you love in your home. You will have fewer decisions to make with fewer items which will lead to an inner calmness. You will also be more organized in a way that transfers to other aspects of your life as well.

Close your eyes and think of your home currently. What is it about the home that is upsetting to you? Is it messy, disorganized, or chaotic? Is it a source of stress and discontent to you? Now, imagine if you were in your home, and it looked just exactly the way it does in the dreams of your ideal home. Imagine soothing aesthetics, a place for every item, and everything where it belongs. The organization and decor provide a serenity that is felt by anyone who enters your home. As you look around, you will see only your very favorite possessions, giving you a chance to truly appreciate them and what they mean to you. There is nothing to distract you from the things that you love. There is no clutter to cause stress or discontent. You would feel calm, relaxed, and in control. These are the feelings that you are moving towards. You are on the right track. You can sort things out and reach your goal of a remarkable home.

A major source of stress in your home is probably the number of things that you own. If you have less, everything can be placed in its own area, or even be out of sight if that is what you wish. With fewer items, there will be less visual chaos and your eyes and mind can be calmer and more soothed. You will have less stress because you will know exactly where everything is at all times. You will never have to second guess where you left your reading glasses or your favorite shoes. By living in a calm environment, you are allowing your mind to have its own sense of calm. This is what will consequently be projected out to others. You will no longer carry the weight of the stress and disorganization of your home with you throughout the day. It will be an amazing feeling to leave your home each day having rested and rejuvenated from spending time in your own personal oasis.

You may project emotions that you do not even realize you are carrying around with you. You might be burdened by constantly searching for items. You may feel overwhelmed at the sheer number of things you possess. Even if these thoughts and feelings are not at the forefront of your mind, you project them to others from a more subconscious level. It might project in a more tangible way such as always having difficulty locating paperwork for meetings or having a hard time keeping track of our schedule. The bottom line is that if you feel any negative emotions from having too much, once you declutter, your entire demeanor can change. The image you put out to the world can be entirely different. You have control over the way others see you. The easy first step is to declutter your life in order to declutter your mind.

Once you feel content with your home, you'll be able to willingly share it with others. You may begin to host dinner parties or hold a movie or game nights with your friends. Your friends and family will appreciate the calm and warm feelings that will emanate to them from a home that contains items for which someone truly cares. In these social situations, the calm and peace radiating from your mind will be impressed upon others. Your guests will be able to tell what the things of real importance are in your life through the decor and items that you have chosen to display in your home. Your personality will be able to shine through your cherished possessions. Your visitors may remark upon how clean, warm, and organized your home is, and they will also feel the same peaceful vibes projecting from you. This is the best version of yourself that you want to present to the world.

Your mantra from this chapter is, "A calm home environment leads to a calm mind. I am in charge of creating my environment, which affects my mind, and therefore, I will project the best version of myself in front of the world."

Chapter 4: Tips to Start Decluttering

There are many theories regarding how you should go about decluttering. Minimalism has become quite trendy within the past few years. There is a multitude of books, videos, television shows, and manuals that can be found that tell you step-by-step on what to do to declutter your items. Yet there are no hard and fast rules. The reality of the situation is that you have to decide how much you need, how much you want to kiss goodbye, and which items are special enough to stay. The remainder of this chapter will present some guidelines and tips that you may wish to refer to in starting your decluttering journey.

A suggestion on how to begin is to pick a room. For example, the kitchen. Start with one corner of the room and move clockwise, from top to bottom, throughout the room. Once the first room has been decluttered, proceed to the second, and so forth, until you have completely decluttered your home. Remember, there is no set timeline in which your decluttering mission has to be completed. Make a rough timetable such as a week and allow yourself breaks if you begin to feel overwhelmed. You may only be able to complete one room on a certain day, and that is alright. As long as you are making progress toward the goal of your dream home, you are on the right track.

It is also helpful to have a destination in mind for the items which you declutter. You may wish to pick a particular charity organization to donate the items. Some options are homeless shelters or resale shops. It can be much easier to part with things if you know where your former possessions are going, and particularly if you know that they will help someone who needs them. You will be able to quickly remove the items from your home so that they no longer cause clutter.

Decide on What You Need and Use

This is a fairly easy step from which you can begin with. The basis of this step is to go through your home and pull out the items for which you no longer have a use. If something has no value in the sense of being a useable or necessary item, it can go. If you have multiples of an item, but clearly favor one, you can let the others go.

Some examples of items you may decide to give away are:

- Extra kitchen appliances
- Unused clothing
- Books you have already read

Decide on What You Cherish

This category will really help you clear out items of faux-sentimental attachments. This is where you can choose which possessions truly make you happy. Do not keep things simply because of who gave them to you or how long you have had them. Take some time and really analyze the feelings you have about each item. If you feel burdened by the item, let it go. If you truly love and cherish the item, allow it to stay.

Some things you may release from this category include:

- Gifts
- Collectible items
- Things you have possessed for a long time

Decide on What You Have Space For

This step is an important one especially if you have a lot of possessions and lack space. For example, if you have only one small closet in your home, it does not make sense to have it overflowing with clothing items and shoes. Once you have cleared out each space of things that have no value to you and that you do not cherish, take the time to organize that area. Everything that you choose to keep needs to have a place of its own. You should know where to find everything and you should be happy and calm when viewing the aesthetics of the room. You may wish to purchase or make dividers for drawers or to add storage in the form of shelves or ottomans made to store possessions. Whatever way you decide to go about this step, make sure that all your possessions have a specific place to rest or be contained. This is also the time that you put your unique touch on your home. This is when you can decide what objects you would like to display.

Some examples of items that you may discover you would like to remove include:

- Knick-knacks

- Large items

- Anything that no longer meets your needs in your space

Quick Tips to Declutter Thoroughly

- Set a plan or goal for each day. Start with one room or even one drawer. Once you get started, you will have the momentum to keep going. Set an end date by which to complete the purge.

- Make a quick round of your home and pick up any clutter. Sort through these items first. You may find that the clutter is trash, things you do not cherish or things for which you no longer have space.

- Stick to one room at a time for thorough decluttering. Finish one room before moving on to the next. It takes a lot more time if you jump from place to place without completion of an area.

- Set up boxes for keeping, donating, and trash. These can be plastic bins, cardboard boxes, garbage bags, or whatever you would like to use. The important thing is to have a designated thing to place the items that are staying and going.

- Limit your stored possessions. The amount you decide on is up to you. You may have space for only one memory box. You may have room to store old children's clothes that you will pass to your younger children. Decide what is appropriate for your situation and set the limit.

- Consider having a garage sale or a yard sale to make some extra cash. You might want to try your hand at selling some items before tossing them. Just be firm in the sense that whatever is left at the end of the sale day leaves your home that day. When the sale is over, either let friends and family choose what they would like to take and pack it up for donating or throw it away.

- If it does not work, toss it. If clothing no longer fits, it needs to be donated to someone who can use it. If something is broken and cannot be used, all it is doing currently is taking up valuable space. Dispose of those items and move on.

- Clear off shelves, counters, and tables. The flat surface has a tendency to be drop zones. They often accumulate papers and other items with no homes. Clear these areas first to see an immediate difference in the aesthetics of your home.

- If it does not belong in the room it is in, either move it away or remove it. As you come across items that are in a room where they do not belong, remove them from that space. Either relocate the items or donate them.

- If it is trash, kiss it goodbye. You really do not need empty boxes and envelopes from the mail. Recycle or trash these items.

- See how much you have of same items, and purge what you do not need. Do you really need 4 curling irons? Are there only one or two that you use? Donate or give the rest away.

- Remove decluttered items from your home as quickly as possible. If you declutter and then let the items sit in your home, you have not really completed the process. The end goal is to get the extra clutter out of your home and out of your life.

- Do a weekly 10-minute declutter just to make sure you haven't slipped up and re-accumulated items. Choose a day and time, perhaps every Saturday morning, and remove any items that have piled up. Put away things you need but were put in the wrong place, and discard anything unneeded.

Your mantra for this chapter is, "I can make informed decisions regarding my possessions. I will keep only things that are useful, cherished, and have a designated home."

Chapter 5: Breaking the Habit

Now, you have learned many tips and strategies for getting started on your decluttering project. Whether you are in the process of planning, have already started, or have completely decluttered your home, it is very important that you do not fall back into old habits that will allow clutter to regain a place in your life. With a few simple steps, you can be sure to break the habit and keep your home in top condition at all times.

Organizing Hacks

The number one way to keep your home looking like the one in your favorite magazine photos is to set up an organization system that works for you and to stick to it. Let's outline a few samples of ways that you can get organized and stay on track. You can choose your favorite or take bits from each to create your own custom system.

One of the major types of clutter is related to paper. These are things such as bills, mail, and receipts. Paper tends to pile up quickly and without warning. There are a few ways to tackle the organization of this type of mess so that it does not get in the way of your happy space. A bullet journal can be used to jot down notes for appointments and bill due dates, as well as to track your schedule. All you really need to get started is a quality notebook and a pen. Make this one place to put anything you may need to look at later such as to-do lists, contact information, and important dates. You may also decide to set up a command center. These work well for families. The kitchen is a great place to set everything up. It is the spot where everyone gathers. You can use the interior of a cabinet to tape up a calendar with everyone's schedules. A file folder can help you sort out mail as it comes in, and gives you a place to stash bills, receipts, and other paper items. You can teach children to place any papers that need to be signed in this area. Grocery lists and weekly menus can also be kept inside a cupboard door for easy access. It is often helpful to keep all important documents in one place. Keep one binder that is dedicated to items such as birth certificates, passports, warranties, and vaccination records.

Another source of clutter involves all of the things that are needed on a daily basis as you leave your home. Try setting up a mudroom that everyone in the home should use as a place to store their shoes, coats, hats, umbrellas, keys, backpacks, and purses. This way, the clutter from the day does not enter the house. It all will have a space near the door. This will also make mornings easier when all that is needed can be easily located. Another positive aspect to having a mudroom is that dirt from shoes will not be scattered through the house thereby allowing you to save time on cleaning up dirt, water, and mud as everyone enters the home. If you have limited space, consider a long bench near the entry or in the garage. Woven baskets can be stored under the bench to store shoes. Hooks can be placed on the wall to hold coats and bags.

Closets are notorious as centers of mess and clutter. You can order closet organization systems online, or find them in many stores. These systems can be adjustable or made to order. You can also create a bit of personal organization with stackable shelving or bins. Stacked bins or small drawers can easily hold undergarments, swimwear, socks, and accessories. This is also a great place to contain workout clothing and pajamas. With wall shelving, you can create a space to hold folded sweaters and jeans, while allowing the hanging space to be dedicated to blouses, work shirts, and trousers. Keeping two lidded hampers in each closet will make for easy sorting of dark and light clothing for the laundry.

There are some general guidelines to follow that will make your life easier and neater. One of the best pieces of advice is to label things. Put a name for each family member on their basket for the mudroom. Label where items go in the kitchen or in children's playrooms. Words or pictures will work fine. If every person sees where items belong, everyone can help keep things in their place. In common rooms such as dens, storage furniture and baskets can contain items neatly while keeping them out of view. Remote controls can be kept in a basket on a bookshelf. Throw blankets or children's toys can be kept in ottomans with lids.

Evening Gathering

Do a little bit of tidying each day. If you wait for the weekend, for example, your clutter will only multiply. Each evening after dinner, do a quick walkthrough of your home. Take a tidying basket with you and gather everything that needs to get back to its assigned home. Make sure to put these items away before you head to bed. If you have family members or roommates, try using a canvas bag for each person's possessions. Then after gathering, the tidying part of putting things away can be easily divided. Each person is then responsible for their own mess. Your home will seem much calmer when you wake up each morning without the mess of the previous day to greet you.

Have everyone who lives in the home pitch in and play a part. Set up a routine cleaning schedule with tasks that need to be accomplished each day. Each person can complete one or two tasks each day as well as his/her works for families or roommates. For example, let's assume that a particular home has four people who are living in it. One person can cook dinner and feed the pet. The second person can be in charge of washing the dishes and watering the plants. A third person could clean the counters and floors, and a fourth could tackle a load of laundry and set the table. You can even utilize a magnet board in your kitchen command center to rotate jobs on a daily or weekly basis. If everyone in the home takes on a small amount of responsibility each day for the tidiness, the home will remain a soothing oasis from the outside world.

Decor

The design and function of your home will contribute to the overall aura that it projects. Everything from the color scheme to the arrangement of your cherished knick-knacks will have an effect on the overall feeling of the home. A neutral color palette is soothing to the eye and exudes a feeling of calmness. Simple lines in furniture will add a cleaner look to the room. A common theme in decorating is to use the rule of three. This is when three objects are grouped together for aesthetic purposes. For example, three small potted plants can be placed together on a shelf, or an end table can be home to a framed photo, a table lamp, and a large gemstone. Try not to crowd things. If there is space between items as your eyes view them, then your body will feel calmer as if you have more breathing room. Natural elements can make a room shine while maintaining a calm atmosphere. Wood, plants or succulents, or a soothing fish tank can be focal points of room design. Natural lighting will give the interior a fresh and soothing feeling. This can be accomplished with sheer curtains, or you could choose to forego curtains altogether and opt only for window blinds. Alternatively, a fireplace will add warmth and coziness, and also be a relaxing focal feature of a home.

Your mantra from this chapter is, "I am the master of my domain. I will create and maintain a truly remarkable home."

Chapter 6: Take Photos and Share with Friends

No matter how hard you try something, there is always a chance of falling back into old habits. To safeguard yourself from letting clutter gather again, you will need to have a plan and some strategies in place to keep your home in its new, beautiful, remarkable state. Digital photos are good for this in many ways. You can keep photos of items, as well as take photos to use as a reference for what your home looks like in its best condition. The great thing about digital photos is that they do not take up physical space or create clutter in your home. The rest of this chapter will discuss some ways in which digital photos can help you keep clutter at bay while providing an incentive to stay on track.

Create a Digital Artwork Portfolio for Your Children

One way to trim down on clutter and prevent it from gathering once again is to take photos of things to keep in your possession digitally, instead of physically keeping those same items. You will be amazed at how well this one simple change works. One of the best places that you can apply this strategy is to children's artwork. Art made by your children is something that you will want to keep forever, in its entirety, but it can take up a lot of space and be notoriously difficult to organize. However, you do not need to part from any of it. A digital art portfolio can be cherished forever and will never add physical clutter to your home, plus it awards you with the opportunity to review all of the art of all of your children at any time you would like. All you have to do is take photos of the artwork currently in your possession and then add photos as new artworks come in. This tactic will also keep each piece of art pristine, without a chance of deterioration. Photos can be stored on your computer, on a zip drive, or in a digital space online. These photos can be emailed or printed out and used as holiday cards to send out to your loved ones. In this way, you can share prized pieces with many people.

Cherish Photos, Not Items

Sometimes you have large, bulky items or possessions that do not add any significant useful value to your life. On the other hand, perhaps you have some of the sentimental or guilt items spoken about earlier in this book. For whichever of the reasons, you have kept these things, now they bring you stress any time you look at them, or whenever the thought of them crosses your mind. You do have control over these items, however. These types of items are another of which you can take photos of to store digitally. You may have an attachment to something, but have no place to store it, or you may like the look of something, but no longer wish to own it. By taking photos of these items, you can look at the photos if you want, but do not have to maintain ownership or deal with the clutter that the item presents. You can also use these photos as memories to look fondly back on with family members and friends.

Keep Digital Copies to Reduce Paper Clutter

Digital copies of owner's manuals can also be a better way to reduce the amount of paperwork that you have lying around your home. More often than not, you probably will not even ever use many of the owner's manuals that you have for appliances and the like. In that case, you just are storing papers that have no practical use and are probably scattered throughout your home. Owner's manuals are one of the most likely items to contribute to clutter because you never know exactly what to do with them or where to keep them. Keeping the manuals digitally will prevent this scenario from happening and adding more clutter to your home. Then, if you ever need to look at a manual for something you own, a digital copy will come in handy.

Share Photos with Friends

Sometimes you hold onto things with the sole intention of showing them to another person such as a friend or coworker. This may be in the form of a flyer that you received in the mail, something you think your friend would find interesting or humorous, or an article from a magazine you would like to share. In some cases, you might keep something you otherwise would not, for quite some time, and may end up not even showing it to the person you intended. You can prevent this from happening by snapping a quick photo and then bidding the item adieu. Smartphones are especially handy for this sort of thing, because you always have your cell phone with you to easily take a quick photo, and then you will also have it with you when you remember to show the item to your friend. You can also consider taking photos of magazine recipes you would like to try or of advertisements of things you would like to purchase. Then you can toss the original item that contained these thereby preventing a build-up of clutter.

Keep Photos for Reference

Once you are done with the process of decluttering your home, you probably will get a lot of pleasure seeing it all organized and decorated to your liking. However, it is also most likely a process full of hard work and quite possibly filled with difficult decisions. You want to be sure that you know and remember what your home looks like in the way that pleases you the most. An easy way to be able to reference your home at its best is to take photos of each room as you finish organizing and decorating it. If you ever begin to lose the sense of calmness and serenity from your new oasis, you can compare the photos of the room to the room's current condition. Then, you will be able to decide if there is anything you need to do to return the room to its former splendor. This can also be beneficial if you decide to redecorate, but decide that you do not like the new look. This way, if you would like to return things to the way they were, you will have a reference photo from which to do so. The photos can also serve as an inspiration to keep you from going back to old ways. If your home begins to get a bit on the untidy side, just take a glance at your beautiful photos, and nip the clutter in the bud.

Share Your Progress through Photos

Finally, a way to utilize digital photos to your advantage is to be able to share your progress. You may wish to take before and after photos to show how far you have come. You can send photos or email digital photos to family members who live far away to show off your remarkably organized and aesthetically pleasing home. If you have never let friends into your home because of the previous clutter, you can share photos as well. You may wish to share ideas of your new interior design or to show them how peaceful your home is. Sharing your photos with others also helps to hold you liable for keeping up the current state of your home.

Your mantra for this chapter is, "I will not fall back into old habits. I will use photos to keep clutter at bay and to share things with friends."

Chapter 7: Maintaining the Mindset

When forming any new habit, maintaining the correct mindset is of the utmost importance. Some of the ways in which to do this are to develop new behaviors, replace old behaviors with new ones, have good intentions to stay on track, and maintain motivation. You must make small changes and create small habits in order to reach the ultimate goal. In this case, the goal is to maintain a clean and clutter-free home. To do so, you must first declutter, and rid your home of any garbage, but it is equally important not to let too much back into your home. You want to avoid a cycle of having too much, decluttering, having a serene home environment, purchasing unneeded items, and then needing to declutter once again. Now that you have the trash out, you want to keep it out for good. In this chapter, you will learn strategies to keep the clutter at bay and to prevent an excessive influx of new items from making their way back into your home.

Weekly Walkthrough

A relatively simplistic approach to keeping clutter down is to take a weekly walkthrough of your home. You should choose a specific day and time slot for this so that it becomes a habit for you to do. It should only take a few minutes if done on a weekly basis.

Perhaps you can choose Saturday mornings so that you can quickly complete the task and have a soothing, clutter-free weekend ahead of you. Take a basket with you and make a mental note of any areas that seem to be cluttered or untidy. Figure out what the cause of clutter is in all of the areas. Do you need a better storage system for your toiletries? Is there an excess of some items that could be purged or donated? Have things been left out for some other reason? Determine the issue and develop a fix. You may decide to add a storage basket under your bathroom counter, move items to the correct location, or to donate or throw away excess items. If you take a few moments of your time once each week, your home will not have a chance to deviate from the newfound calm and peaceful state you have created.

Charity Box

Another easy way to keep your possession spared down is to keep a charity box. This could be a sturdy board box, a storage crate, or anything you would like it to be. You have options of where to keep it as well, but make sure it is always in the same place so you and your family members can find it. You may choose to keep it in the trunk of your car, on a shelf in the garage, or in the basement. Whenever you come across an item that you no longer need or want, it should go directly into the charity box. Make sure that it is in good condition and in good working order. Otherwise, it just goes into the garbage can. If you purchase a new coffee maker, the old one goes immediately into the charity box. If you replace your running shoes, the old ones go in the charity box. Anything that can still be used by someone else, but no longer has value to you goes in the charity box. You can take items to a homeless shelter or to a charity shop once a month, or whenever the box is full. If you know of someone personally who could use the items, you can check to see if they would like the one you are getting rid of. You can also try to sell some of the items. You could have a garage sale or try your hand at online auction sites. Whatever you choose to do, just remember that once something goes in the charity box, it cannot come back into your home.

An additional option with the use of the charity box is to get the whole family involved in a game. You can do this seasonally for optimum results. Set the box in a central location and set a timer. See how many unnecessary items each member of the family can bring to the charity box before the timer goes off. Let the winner choose something fun such as a family outing for the day. You could also let the winner choose the charity to which you will donate the contents of the box. This will not only help keep the clutter down, but will also teach children that giving to others can bring good feelings. You will be instilling good values and teaching them that they do not have to receive their joy from possessions.

Do Not Bring in Things You Do Not Need

This part is about creating new shopping habits. You do not want to get your home to a point where it is completely clutter-free and well organized just to bring in too many things once again. In order to break the cycle and embrace the new clutter-free mindset, there are some questions that you should ask yourself anytime you are considering an item for purchase. If you answer in the negative to all of these questions, you do not have a reason to purchase the item and bring it into your home. The new item will be unneeded and cause clutter. It will also not be bringing value to your life. This does not apply to things such as groceries, but to non-necessary items such as when you are shopping for fun.

Ask yourself, "Do I love it?" This is a good place to start. If the object is not something that you love, then it does not deserve a place in your home among your cherished items. You will not enjoy having it take up extra space, nor will you cherish it. If you do love the item, ask yourself, "Do I have space for this in my home?" If you do not have space for it, then you probably should not purchase it. You will want to avoid purchasing anything that will add to clutter in your home. If you have answered positively to the first two questions, proceed by asking yourself, "Do I have anything else like this at home already?" For instance, if you already have a plaid blazer at home, do you really need another one? If it is something you truly cannot live without, then, for further

43

clarification, ask yourself, "Am I willing to donate the one I already have?" This will help you to determine if you really do love the item at the store as much as the one you currently own, or if the one you possess is the better option. Finally, ask yourself, "Do I need this item?" If you find that you do not need the item, then you already know that it does not need to make its way into your home. After decluttering, you do not want to bring anything into your home that is unneeded or without value.

In mastering these new habits, you will be able to maintain the right mindset to keep your home in its remarkable condition. You will be able to live in an environment where there is less stress and have a decluttered home that brings you happiness and serenity. That is one of the best things that anyone could ever ask for.

Your mantra from this chapter is, "I have control of what enters and exits my home. I will form new habits to maintain my new lifestyle in the home I love."

Conclusion

Thanks for making it through to the end of *7 Steps for Minimalism Declutter: How to Create a Remarkable Home and Kiss Your Trash Goodbye*. Let's hope it was informative and able to provide you with all the tools you need to achieve your goals whatever they may be.

The next step is to get started on the clutter in your home! Remember to start and finish one area at a time. You will be so motivated after the first room that you will be jumping at the chance to finish your home. Donate, sell, and declutter your way to the home you have always dreamed of. Scale things down and decorate for a soothing and relaxing sanctuary from the outer world.

Create your systems of organization and stick to them to maintain the mindset of keeping a clutter-free and remarkable home. Whether you opt for creating organization stations throughout your home or call in professionals to design them for you, utilize your space in the best ways possible and keep your possessions in their new homes. Check back on your photos to motivate you to keep the tidiness up.

Once you have finished your decluttering, remember to get everyone in on the responsibility of maintaining your dream home. Schedule chores and have everyone lend a hand. It is so much easier if everyone pitches in. It will not even feel like work to keep things maintained.

Finally, if you found this book useful in any way, a review on Amazon is always appreciated!

Renae K. Elsworth

Made in the USA
Columbia, SC
02 January 2019